RICHARD M. BEST

# THE BASKET WEAVER

POEMS

Tellwell Talent
www.tellwell.ca

ISBN
978-1-77370-947-5 (Paperback)
978-1-77370-948-2 (eBook)

*Dedicated to my family*
*&*
*In memory of my father, Mascoll MacDonald Best*

# CONTENTS

# CONTENTS CONT'D

# CONTENTS CONT'D

# A SOLDIER - FOREVER YOUNG!

You did not hear –
The cries of the one –
Who suffered a bruised knee,
Nor with your pursed lips,
Blow away the fragment –
From a child's painful –
Tearfilled watery eye;
You were not there –
To extract the splinter –
From an aching finger;
Nor to lend an ear –
To the ways of an errant child;
Nor to whisper a 'tender goodnight' –
After a busy, busy day;
Nor to chide for his/her –
Misdemeanour!

But mother-dear was –
Everything we had,
And she did smother us,
With love and tender kindness –
For her, and for 'you beyond'!

We could not ask…
For greater or for more…
And this even up until…
And to way past three score –
And more!

Your 'Grands', your 'Great-grands' –
Indicative of your brief sojourn here,
They…your meaningful journey,
A testament of your passage.

And to realize – that now…
You reside, a shining star,
In the vast firmament;
Referred to – remembered…
Revered…always, and forever!
For – though you 'be gone'…
Yet - you be a constant in our life!
A soldier – forever young!

# THE MAPLE LEAF

Every hill and valley,
Bathed in its luxurious flirtation –
Unapologetic intrusion into
Our very psyches;
Replicated times over, in
Our pale pretentious canvassed
Reproduction of nature's gift –
This leaf – we call 'Maple'.
Ubiquitous -plenteous,
In shameless exhibition,
Its green-red-gold –
Inevitable explosion of
Colour of every hue,
Every complexion
Bid adieu –
But –
Shall be retained couch-clasped
Between pages, and within the bosom
Of a favoured lexicon-
Our erudition…
A reminder –
At season's end –
The Maple shall return…
Evermore flamboyant,
Evermore plenteous,
Evermore evergreen,
Evermore Canadian,
Then always – and,
Evermore…
The First of July!

## ABOUT POETRY

There is poetry...and then...
There is...
Poetry!!
Poetry...brief and
genuine...enlightening...
Poetry...in quantity...
elaborating...embracing...
Much is elucidating...
engaging...elevating...
Much is fabrication...
obfuscation...protraction...

In it's seduction...
Courting us into galloping...
Rambling circumlocution!
How much is remembered?
How much is forgotten?
What should be remembered?
What should be forgotten?
Much should be remembered...
For so much could be
forgotten!!

## ITS MAKING

With every deliberate, meditative footfall,
The poem beckons from beyond –
Erupting with volcanic intensity – or
Descends in the misty clouds of thought…
Hugging the mountain top of imagination…
And lingers…and lingers…
Refusing to go away – disappear…
Be off! Be done! Be gone! Oh…bother!

This thought that persists - insists -
Its revelation held in abeyance,
But will find its moment of truth –
After all the processing…
Bordering on neglect –
Refusing to go away,
Begging the question -
Whether or not…to be –
Finds itself scattered across the page –
And then…
Is!

## AS A MOTHER WOULD...

She would brush away the tears
Her reassuring embrace would –
Tell that all would be well...
After we had come limping in –
The aftermath of a bruised knee...
Wincing from a fragment in a tear-filled eye –
All during...
The course of a child's 'normal day'.

A few words from her -
Was all it would take,
To know that we are secure –
And would fear no more...
For who else can chase –
The cares away of...
A sometimes wicked world out there.

Who could...as a mother would –
Keep the wolves at bay...
Only a mother dear...
Only a mother's care.

This tranquillity – this calm...
Engendered by the magical...
Gentle stroking of her comforting hand...
It is only with the passage of time...
It will all come back to you.

# THE OUTSIDER

Helpless, helpless is the condition – while,
In that other room –
A body is assailed by,
Urgent proddings of young life –
Birth pangs – no less;
Her feelings, the bitter sweet pain –
Of motherhood,
That can never be explained.

We nod 'understandably', but
Can never fully comprehend,
The female experience,
As we gloat in our –
Masculine futility.

## 'DREAM PILLOWS'

Sandwiched between these
Now 'stained' pillows…
Over the years – when
Very young heads –
Would lie awake,
Chattering way into the night
Of dreams and of 'things to be' -
Of dragons to slay –
And of flowers to gather;
Of castles they would build,
Of oceans to cross –
Of lives to be lived – and
Of lives they would give –
To the next generation.

Now this bald and greying head –
Would sometimes lie awake…
And think of how lucky…
How fortunate…how blessed…
As parents we are –
To witness some semblance –
Of some dreams come true;
Of promises fulfilled –
Of steady steps – with
Only so much advice…
With a future – a life
And…
Theirs to discover…

# THIS STREET

This street...that –
Goes this...and that way...
This two-way street –
Meeting him and her...
And where I meet you...
And you meet me –
As daily travelled...
By me...by you!
And to think that -
They are some – who
Would have you – me
To think...believe it – to be
A one-way street!
This street of tolerance –
Remains a vital conduit –
Of free ideas for him – for
Her...
For you – for me...
A freeway of ideas...yours
And mine;
Thoughts exchanged in this –
Corridor of expectations...
Among all of every hue...
You and me...me and you!
No cul-de-sacs this!
But back and forth...
And back...again!
This tolerance...this
Two-way-street – holds.
Promises – no stagnation here
No secrets sought – just

Clarity…
As plain to see…
By you…by me –
So be it…So let it be…

## ON THIS CORNER

It's a beautiful day today…
As I stand here on this corner;
How many mornings have I stood here…
Watching the break of dawn…
Waiting for some means of getting to town –
Where for seven and some hours a day –
The job devoured the time…the time…
The time that I have so much of now;
On this corner faces were strained at first –
Then the odd smile…as we became familiar –
With the same hour of arrival and the waiting…
On this corner;
A sort of 'family gathering' so to speak…
Then the –'Hi Harry'! – 'Good-morning Charles'…
'How are you Emily'?
Regardless of the climate!
But that was some time ago – and yet –
As if it were only yesterday…yesteryear;
The faces became fewer…older –
Once pliable clay – now…sun-baked and –
Set in pleasing contours that spell –
Earlier pleasant, agreeable happy times…
Times that led up to this moment of contentment –
To be reflected on with gratitude…
For being part of that family –
On this corner;
But wait!  That figure crossing the street:
Could it be Harry?  No!  Could not be!
For Harry is almost twice forty…
Certainly fooled me…
The rolling shoulders and lumbering gait –

Almost tempted to say 'Hello'!
On second thought –
Would not want to have him break his stride –
Have him pay attention to – and
Not to recognize –
My once...familiar gesture...
And the lady...the lady beside him...
So much like Emily...
So many years before...
I wonder...how is Harry?
Ah well...the sun is past noon-hour...
I'd better be getting back –
Shouldn't leave Isabelle alone for too long;
Will stop at the pharmacy for the medication...
Then hurry home for that cup of coffee –
Perhaps...just perhaps...
Isabelle remembers Emily and Harry...
Nice day though...
Ah well...
Until tomorrow...

# TRUTH?

And the debate is on…
Whether this or that –
Whether this is – or…
It is not!
And to and fro…and back –
And then back again –
The debate is on…
Some elucidation…some clarification –
But…but within –
An almost natural inclination
The concomitant…almost –
Inevitable obfuscation!
Winners and…or losers
But…but…the truth?
Where is it in this play –
Of and on words…this –
Elusive creature –
The truth!
Slippery as – slippery -
Would be…as we wrestle
With the if's…and but's –
And the why's…the wherefore's –
Then perhaps and the maybe's
And…and – then whatever!
This constant search for –
Clarity…lucidity…but –
Deep within – and beneath…
And under camouflage –
The truth lurks…waiting –
To be discovered!

## DANK DAY

The gloom…the gloom…
Will it lift by noon…
Or so we think…and hope…
And pray –
That this thin veil of overcast gray –
Be punctured by a sun-ray soon!
As late as only yesterday…
Had fair warning of today –
But…it is now – way past infancy…
And we have witnessed the prophecy!
Had it not complied as prophesied…
We would say –
'They lied!!'
Accept each day for what it is…
No fabrication – man calls his!
A product from pre-determined source…
Enjoy the best…and brave the worst!
But all is not lost in many ways –
There're more tomorrows…
Todays…and yesterdays!
And so…in their diversity…
From here on…into eternity!
Some days like this…
Some days like that!
C'est la vie…
C'est ma vie!!

## LAST GASP?

Now snuggly seated on this numbered VIA Car
Mississauga – Montreal bound –
This train hurries its way across –
A frowning terrain –
Signs of the last vestiges of another –
Winter with images of tired-
Spec-filled patches of –
Burnt-brown-snows...here and there
Exhausted from cold suffocation.
All slipping rapidly by –
As this train slices its way...
Its 'hooting – haunting' refrain on –
Approaching intersections...and 'swoosh' –
As these faint ghostly – sounds drift pass into –
The evening's dusky light...and
This landscape – a partially frozen tundra –
Now on the wane...

Here and there leafless trees of dark brown –
Winter's legacy – and
Like mighty oaks with arms out-stretched skywards
In beseeching supplication for a warmer clime...
When starlings will fill their green branches
While emitting their peculiar symphonies...

A time when the staccato-rhythmic greetings –
Of – 'Hi! – Hello!  Salut!'
With the display of open-neck shirts – and
The varied colours of ladies skirts – that
Will flutter in gentle breezes –
As we wistfully ponder...
Spring...

The Season ahead…
Witnessing the last grasp –
Last Gasp?
Of a Winter –
That has gone –
That-a-Way!!

# NORTH POINT

As if standing on the tip of the earth,
As far as the eye can see,
Skirting pale blue horizon,
A peaceful picture to behold,
Tranquil…still…except for -
The whistle of the wind.

Vision uninterrupted,
Makes glutton of this scene;
Wide expanse of glistening sea,
Myriad white-caps,
Bobbing stealthily.

Drink this scenery,
Brief medicine for melancholy,
Choke back the sob of gratitude,
For having sampled–
One brief moment of eternity.

The wave full blown,
Then belated gesture,
Shows fluffy white plume,
Then full crescendo –
Crashes headlong against the shore,
Registers foamy signature once more,
On these dark-brown jagged tablets –
Monuments to the parent of –
This child – this coral isle.

Crashes way down on rocks below,
The cacophony – then orchestration,
Growls in its caves,
Once more to explore –

With darting wet silvery effervescent tongues,
Make successive overlapping –
Parabolic design on brown sands,
Slithers back, in its elasticity.

Bright noon-day sunbeams,
Make celestial display,
With full spectrum rainbow,
In particles of sea-spray.

Closing eyelids, feel the –
Damp caress of salty air,
Be intoxicated by free ozone,
Gulp freely – transcend all time,
Smell – taste that salty perfume –
A sudden rebirth!

Words cannot explain
So inadequate, so mundane –
Go enjoy the same –
For you see…for me, now –
It's just a memory!

# WHEN?

Somewhere along the way –
We pause – retrace our steps,
And count the hill tops
Where once we stood –
Scanning peaks and valleys…
Wondering which had been worth the while
And which had not –
Trying to recall our greatest triumph.

If done with honesty,
Becomes even harder to determine;
Each will say –
'No! Not this…yes…that!
Or, is it the other way around?
Or, perhaps…the time is not yet.

How do we measure the circumstance?
At what point can we –
Without fear of contradiction,
Shout from that vantage point –
'I have arrived'!
And same time to escape –
Resounding echoes,
In valleys below –
Reverberating –
'It's a lie…It's a lie!'

# QUINTESSENTIAL QUÉBECOIS

It was the soul,
That shone though
His smoldering eyes;
Always there...
Hardly, and if ever,
And seldom sent an attaché.

Reachable, approachable –
Lending an ear of –
Understanding;
Always there...

Poet, philosopher,
Humanitarian, politician,
Person of the people,
Fiercely fair, in his
Deliberations...

He created the space
For you...for me...for almost –
Everyone...
The quintessential –
Québecois!
He was, and is...
Gérald Godin.

# A LIFE

To dwell in that
Narrow corridor of
Personal ambition,
Wealth and acquisition, and –
Disregard for others...
Is to miss the point of –
Our mission here.

To live fully,
Is to dwell on...
Our –
Common humanity –
With, or without
Politics –
Our –
Common humanity –
With, or without
Religion.

# A PLEA (PRAYER)

Let the time be –
Not too far,
Let it happen –
Where you are…
That this dove,
Will find it safe…
To flutter freely –
In the air
To have this dove,
Eventually – and much sooner,
To dutifully settle –
The Ribbon of Peace –
Around and –
About your shoulder.

# 'ONCE UPON A TIME'

It's early in the morning,
No sound of the morning rooster,
No sound of the bleating sheep –
The long-horned goat in parody.

No sound of happy laughter,
Familiar voices on the corner,
Scurrying feet, city bound,
Varied tones of bicycle bells.

I do not hear soprano –
'Sea-eggs…!  Get your sea-egg!'
Don't hear the slow deliberate rumble…
Of the bread-cart wheels,
Those faint drifting smells of-
Fresh baked dough –
Hot 'salt' bread, buns –
And the 'tennis' loaves.

Still listening for, the
Shrill, sharp sound of a whistle
Blown in its peculiar way –
By expert lips – that say,
'Come buy fresh bread to start the day!'
Such a great feeling to be alive –
Can't wait to join vibrant life outside.

## 'BIMSHIRE' BEAMS

At this time…the first cock crows,
As streams of sunlight
Cast long shadows of jalousies
Along the drawing-room floor.

At this time…the air is fresh – unspoiled;
At this time…the splash of water on pillow wrinkled
faces -
At this time…feed time at the barn –
The 'mooing' cow – lazily chewing residuals,
In anticipation, its turn at the fodder basket.

The first sparrows drop to the ground-
For morning crumbs;
At this time…the stirring traffic,
Breaks the morning grace.

At this time…on cool asphalt,
Wet footprints of early swimmers,
Returning from a shallow seaside –
The light-house flashing – at this time,
Soon to be eclipsed by the eternal fire.

To squint at the morning sun, at this time;
The dawn is breaking –
There is an awakening –
At this time…
In Barbados.

## Y/OUR TIME

So precious few –
Those moments allotted us,
And flashing neon-sign, spells…
'Here Today!  Gone Tomorrow!'
'Here Today!  Gone Tomorrow!'

Let us today, think and do…
Those kind thoughts – deeds
Not expressed –
Until too late –
Much, much too late!
The regret – that…
Perhaps had we said –
Or…
Done it, sooner!

The time allotted –
Is to do…and –
Say it now!

Not later!

## TRUTH OR ILLUSION

And…
To dismiss out of hand –
His or Her opinion – is
The ultimate indiscretion!
For none knows for sure – of
The highway to heaven.

We shall live our –
Own private, personal illusion…then –
Let us live our own illusion.

For who has the truth,
Indeed –
Who knows the reason;
Then keep the veil,
Slightly…shyly parted,
Then –
Let the mind be open – for
Some fresh, shared revelation,
And…so…then…
Let us live its possibilities,
To the fullest…
And then to live – our truth,
Our own illusion.

# THE PARTY

And the tinkling of the glasses,
And the groups of heads
In knotted clusters across the room,
And the – 'How do you do?'
And the nodding acquaintance,
And the talk of the weather –
The tennis game –
'Golf tomorrow?'
And now is the time,
In the cool of the night,
Betrayal signs of shoulder straps,
The sun-worshipper's badge.

The murmuring voices
Silver trays of delicacies,
The many choices,
With dainty finger tips
And actor's flair
Pluck expertly from such variety.

And the murmuring –
And – 'Your credentials please?'
In the schooled practices of,
These societies;
Then – 'May we talk?'
Said in so many ways.

The murmur has slowed,
The mumbling has died,
Who has the truth?
Who has lied?

And the last jolly bunch has left…
Jostling, guffawing down the steps;
Last traces of dying champagne,
Dilly-dally in stemmed glasses;
Quiet roar of engines, and…
Boisterous laughter fade into the night.

The door comes shut…
Only to hear faint scratching,
Of Koko's clever paw;
Comes in to rest beside –
Glowing embers of the fireside.

Stretches…yawns…scratches himself,
As if to ask, 'What was that all about?'
Attempt to answer his steady gaze…
Then…break sequence;
Tossing stocking-feet up…on cool divan,
And now…to ponder the sparkle,
In a solitary glass of wine.

## "I-DEN-DITTY"

And the mood is – uncertain…
As the smile – the scowl
This tentative approach – as
To how we shall greet each – and
One another in this multicultural melange;
Regardless of the features –
Regardless of the religion-
Regardless of the complexion – the hue
How shall I greet you?

As we aim to be –
Linguistically, phonetically correct –
Ah! But the accent!
As we stumble – mumble – stammer…
Over one another…
Trying to get it – just right!

As we –
In this never ending song and dance,
This hesitancy…
Comment ca va?  Comment allez-vous?
Or is it to be…
How are you?

This stammer – stumbling –
That harness our spontaneity,
Forcing us to swallow our initial intention;
Our overture – now circumspect,
As we ask – who is he?   Who is she?
Who are they?  Who in fact – are we?
What shall we shed?  What shall we inhabit?
What shall we adopt?...
In this now multi-and-bilingual,

Kébec – Kanadian – Konfusion…
Konundrum!

# CARING HANDS

Oblivious, we chart the course...
Ploughing the fields of endeavour...
Mapping our way to here, or there –
In pursuit of goals – ambition's measure;
But...but then...we may trip –
Stumble, fall along the way -
Our foot caught – twisted awkwardly,
On the footpath to where ever;
It is then... those caring hands are there,
The many as a safety net – to
Catch us!  Not to coddle – but with
Severe attention...take charge!
Administer, apply, sustain the life-line –
To see us on our feet –
To keep us away from -
The edge of the precipice.

## SLUMBER ON...

To bed...to bed...to bed now –
After a busy...busy...day,
Tucked in their beds of
Cool sheets and secure blankets,
These sleepy heads rest comfortably-
Hands clasp between pillow and cheek.

Peaceful is the night – where,
Some moments ago I heard of
Adventures of the day, now...
Peaceful is the night.

Their world concerned partly with toys,
Day by day the questions arise;
Where answers are approximation,
They seek doubtless confirmation,
No escape in compromise –
Thirsting for some satisfaction, now...
Peaceful is the night.

Now they're off in that other world –
Of 'butterflies and monsters'...
I'm sure to learn of escapades
First thing at the breakfast table, now...
Peaceful is the night.

Weary of news of mayhem, chaos and confusion,
Welcome their stories – some fresh revelation;
There's something new under the sun, how...
Peaceful is the night.

## 'THE DEEP'

You...the sea.
Whence, we did come
You...the mystery –
With now calm and –
Shimmering surface – as we,
On raised heels and tip-toe
Lean farther forward –
Casting our shadow across
Your calm and reflective waters;
Attempting to peer into your fathomless depths –
To discover your secrets –
Locked way down deep,
Among the natural castles,
Of crystal coral – where
Resides the flat-backed, flat-bottomed manatee –
Slumbers softly on shifting sand-floors,
Undisturbed by the fitfully fleeting –
Mischievous, restless – darting –
To and fro 'lectric eel;
While...way down deep –
Waiting to be discovered...
Waiting to reveal...
The reasons for life,
Waiting to surrender –
The prescription for longevity –
Flirting, courting watery-way,
Beckoning...
Waiting to welcome us –
Back into eternity.

## 'SMOKEY' - A GENTLE GIANT

On this Friday morning...
After Summer, Autumn, Winter –
And...now Spring...
It is 'minus 14' and a –
'Wind-chill' of 'minus 28' –
To freeze our tears...
Forcing us to pause –
To reflect on your passage here...

For you left us yesterday –
To think of those mornings – those evenings,
When we would be out – and about...
Weather permitting – and you,
To do nature's bidding...
As with smoke in misty eyes –
You came into our lives –
A complete stranger...
And then...took over our lives –
Not long after;

Your presence was...
Always reassuring –
You were never boring,
We took note of –
The hint in your 'woof-bark' -
Perked ears – 'tail-wag-swish'
And would wonder at –
Your next canine wish – and
In frequencies only you could hear...
You would warn us if danger was near;

But you were always in our plans,
And easy to be with...

Stepping around you – and about you,
Was a dancer's delight;

Your weighty wonderful -
Friendly, frolicking nudge – that
Pointed us in some direction –
As you nestled you giant –
Gentle body into any one,
Favourite corner to snooze…
Or maybe snore…
These are the memories –
You left us…
For evermore…

# THE BASKET WEAVER

Words...words...words...
Belief...belief...belief...
We believe – what we believe –
And so be it...and so we be...
For we are –
What we believe...
And then...there's...
The Mantra!
And is it not –
A matter of interpretation...
Whether yours or mine...
Or his or hers?
And to find that this is –
Merely an intellectual exercise of ideas –
Yours and mine;
For whose dogma shall prevail
And whose shall fail –
To capture the minds of the many?
And what shall be –
The ultimate result?
And who shall benefit –
And who is fit to fail?
And who shall make the measurement?
And who shall call into question –
My belief to be it-
And yours is not?
It is...indeed all to the one –
Who tells the story - the mystery evolved...
From one's perspective – and one's interpretation...
As we then...
With heads bent – intent...

To weave our particular basket –
Our own version of events –
Perceived or imagined...
Intent to convince all and some
To consider that...our particular basket –
Would indeed – in fact –
Be...the only one –
To hold the grain...
To hold the water!
Perception...interpretation and
Belief...the engine that drives us!
Whenever...wherever...and –
Always...as we consider –
The Basket Weaver...
Looking in the mirror...

# NOW

Make the most of the moment,
Of life that is here;
For this moment is now,
You dare not count on more.

The future may hold better or worse,
But now, is the moment of life –
That is sure.

Identify where in life's journey
You are –
Then live in the present,
One day at a time.

Take a look!
See...
What happens now – and
Listen to the sounds of the moment;
Smell the fragrance of life –
That is all around – and
Drink in the glory of
Nature's wonderment!

Do it now! Not tomorrow! Not sometime!
For now – is the time to do...
What you must do...
Now is the time of life – and
Now is the time for you –
To be you!

# AN EVENING STROLL

Faint sounds as toads croak in a distant pond;
The idly dropped pebble...
The visible transmission of soundless ripples –
Tier enthusiastic beginning...
Then sneak into the peripheral twilight shade –
Of dark green mossy banks;

Over-hanging trees, and rugged branches –
Hold aloft, thick, rich tropic verdure,
Casting giant shadows across a silent emerald pool;
The air is livened by occasional twitter of –
A restless bird...in search of its ideal perch
For the evening;

The rustle of dry leaves –
As multi-coloured crabs of every description,
Dart about in every direction,
Finding their particular abode –
Leaving tattooed, tell-tale design –
In their hasty departure, to rest secure –
In folds of warm gently undulating white sands;

Soon it will be cool...
And the last traces of this twilight hour,
Will multiply itself times over –
Reflected by ubiquitous grape-leaf –
Heavy with the evening's dewdrops;

Fishing boats, now free for the day,
Rest off-shore, sway...
Lazily on gentle waves...
Lapping at their mossy underside...

As grating anchor-chains –
Make quiet conversation;

Be still...
Glance over your shoulder,
Make casual survey of this –
Bewildering ethereal spectacle -
And feel...
The strange quivering sensation –
Steal up the spine, and spreading –
Its chilly remark...manifests itself –
In warm glow at the nape of the neck;

This indefinable guilt...this wonder!
What have we done –
To deserve...such splendour?

## A CITY SLEEPS

Minutes past mid-night...and –
Slight 'tinkering–sound' of teacup on saucer...
And looking from the 'twenty-first-floor'...
Way...down...down...downwards –
Through these wintry windows...
Buffeted by whistling winds;

The sight of strings of clustered lights –
That dutifully guard the night...
As this city sleeps...
How restful...how peaceful...
No busy-body – to interrupt...
The blessedness of sleep;

Now sleep you – who will and – or
Will not dream of ambition's will...
For tomorrow...and for most –
The sun will rise and cast –
Its multitudinous rays upon –
Our hopes...
Our dreams...
But now...
The tranquility is almost –
Overwhelming in its silence...
As if in anticipation...
Tomorrow's ventures – challenges –
To meet on this other day;

But for now...it is –
Sleep...sleep that will conquer all...
That will refresh... and succour –
That will prepare...replenish –
One and all – and for us –

That we may face...
Another day!!

## THIS BEACON

You – seemingly a monument
Of hope…inspiration…possibilities…
As if at the centre of our universe –
You – this mountain…that is Montreal –
A beacon – regal in splendour…
And beckoning…
Casting your spell…unobtrusive –
And as a silent sentinel –
Monitor our every move…
Courting us at every turn…
As we go about our ways…
Cascading off you –
Rivulets of rich mix and texture –
Around…over…and about you…
Keeping us in check –
Ever mindful…that you –
Are there…we gaze up…and –
You echo the seasons –
Standing full flower – or,
Clothed in pristine snows…
All it takes to know that –
We may go…but –
You – your majesty…
Will hopefully stay –
And will always –
Be there!

# TROPIC DUSK

No more the frothy display,
Now almost dusk, end of another day,
Once billowy shallows, now they subside…
Give way to the rising tide;

Listen to the broken silence –
The persistent beckoning of crickets in the distance;
Waves lapping languidly with curled lips,
Sample the flavour of this coral biscuit;

Blazing sun in reluctant departure –
Its last rays at horizon's rim,
Explodes 'red – orange – purple' in grand-finale,
Torpedoes last beams towards the shore –
Tracing bright scintillating briny paths –
A promise for tomorrow.

# THIS CONCEPT

And lauding such as nirvana
This advocacy for democracy
Seemingly realized by some –
Eluded by some and the other…
How does it come about?
Who makes the determination?
By what measure – circumstance
Can there be the revelation –
That such be the condition –
The realization?
How do we aspire?
How do we proceed?
What is the process – if
Indeed there be only one?
And when have we arrived?
Is it in the form of – or
Through evolution?
Perhaps…revolution?
Or…or…by invasion!
Who will promote…nurture…
Can such aspirations be shaped –
Forcefully from without…or –
Soberly from within?
Can such be through meaningful –
Selfless enticement…
Democracy for its own sake –
Of its own accord?
To stand as universal…
To be proffered at will…or –
For the taking…unconditional?
A concept to be celebrated…

A concept to be yearned for...
A concept – not an instrument
Not to be conveniently distorted...but –
To be imbibed...to be less administered...
To be without brand –
To be without ownership –
By whose authority – by what criteria?
This business...whither democracy!
Be on guard for what may be –
Done in the name of...
That it be used...and not abused!
Donning such garb – and trumpeting –
As 'holier than thou' – then marching into –
Near or far-off distant lands...foreign –
To the concept...
And to some...as strange –
Then to wreak havoc –
In the name of...and
The ensuing...travesty –
A mockery...an abomination!
Autocracy...as democracy...
Bordering on hypocrisy!
Yes...
Democracy...a process...
Not a commodity...sadly...
Accessible to so few...seemingly –
Almost entirely...
Beyond the grasp of –
The Many!!

# THE CATALYST

In their digging…
This drama in the making
Searching for an odour
Some malcontent – attempting
To contaminate your claim
To higher ground;
Their dubious machinations found
One Jeremiah – who would…
Inadvertently give rise to
The national angst…their
Seeming lack of – sister…
Brotherhood…hence…
Nationhood!
And from the highest podium

You would articulate –
The question of the ages…
A veritable declaration…
Our collective Human Rights
The auspices of the –
Damnable…venerable…
The Reverend J. Wright…
As faith…and fate -
Would have it!
In the right place…
At the right time!
Spellbound we were…with
Scarce a moment to spare –
We…sister, brother and –
Many another settled in -
Transfixed by his stature…
And to bear witness…to hear

This misperceived as neophyte who
Would speak as of one –
Of the sages – coming down –
Thrust into the twenty-first Century...
This...now...our moment in time!
This one who transcends –
Continents – ancient and 'new'
Then there...now here...
Obama...America...
Addressing the time – worn...
Blood soaked message of the ages...
Man's inhumanity to man...
To be contemplated...
Denunczated...
Every step we make...
Every breath we take!

## "THE HIGH SEAS"

As we go about our daily chores,
There is...lurking...floating beneath –
The surface...the subconscious,
The roar of the restless waves,
The crash and thunder of an angry sea;
The serenity of a breaking dawn,
After – what had been before...
A day of restless waters – where
Buffeted and thrown – hither and yon;
And on the bow, the breaking foam,
Fore and aft – stem to stern...

The images of a button-down hatch,
Fastened – lashed to-at-times, a...
Free-spinning wheel...this way then that...
Punishing – unrelenting in its uncertain madness!
Backward...now forward spin –
Then momentary – the vessel, birdlike –
As it falls through the air – off...
The crest of yet, another receding swell...reveal-
ing...
A random rudder, like the broken wing,
Of a bewildered albatross – trying to catch the wind;
And a bare naked keel – awkwardly
Seeking a solid wave to carve-slice
Its way through a purposeful nautical mile,
The vessel free-falls, with
A sickening thud into the valley – left by
A departing wave – then swamped by –
Succeeding swell, with sails argumentative...
Snapping their displeasure in haughty gales.

The thought of one of our very own,
Who dares to fulfill the secret of –
Our wildest of wild dreams – who now…with –
Once thick tousled black locks that caught the brisk
salty air…
Now plastered sluicing wet against a mighty fur-
rowed brow –
Anguished – finds comfort in the coddled –
Foetal protective posture against…and within waters
–

Crashing – swirling across well washed decks.

Anxiously…we await some sign
The blip on the screen – a crackling sound,
From…the now battered megaphone…
Anything! anything…that would warn, alert…
Be a balm to our now raw nerves;
That would calm our fears – rising –
To the roofs of anxious anticipation;
When we can expect to run down –
To shores' end – to embrace,
To welcome you in –
From off an indifferent sea,
Back from a hero's journey,
Back from a briny odyssey.

## "DI - ALMOST A QUEEN AND MUCH MORE..."

This Queen of hearts –
This doe-eyed beauty,
This fawn who took our pain –
But could not quench her own;
This butterfly who made –
Every continent her neighbourhood,
Who touched with comfort,
Every type and every stripe;
This princess of privilege and pain,
We selfishly would hope – that
You would see us through it all.

You taught a dynasty –
The rudiments of humility...
To touch, to bend, to hug, to kiss, to care and cry;
To empathize...
To be human, to be vulnerable –
To be like him, like her – like you, like me;
You are a rarity in this fallow land.

You left us a powerful legacy –
In your graceful...elegant – shy modesty;
And as a mother, wife and lover spurned,
To recognize – and to see –
The differences between and among,
Pain, pleasure, truth, honesty and...hypocrisy.

You taught us not to take for granted...
The flowers in the garden of our dreams;
And if plucked...
Then to be tended just as carefully,
With sprinkling care –
The long-stemmed carnations –

Sitting in the base of the mantle;
To tread softly – and
To smite the enemy – the enemy,
That is complacency – that is indifference.

Pursued…hounded by the greedy,
Wretched and the reckless…
The drunken chariot and all came –
To a crashing – untimely halt!  Deep…
Within the entrails of a fabulous –
City of romance; Paris
A veritable, horrible fairy-tale conclusion.

Princess pursued by jackals, their
Bulging blood-shot eyeballs –
Panting…salacious, dripping saliva –
And as if in flight into the mysterious night –
An appointment with some horrible…- horrible
magic hour!

Flash-popping bulbs…
And…and…in a sickening crescendo!

And really…there is no finality;
You taught us how to love…and to lose…
And to love…and to love…again!

## ARLENE & MATTHEW

And then I wondered…
And now I know why –
I seemed to be looking…
Always towards the sky…
As if there be a message drifting by…

And then…You…yes…You…
Caught my eye…and…I Yours –
And nothing would ever be the same!!
It was as it were…
A Celestial Symphony – that
Would transcend space and time –
Writ large among the stars!!

Given this fantastic Canadian landscape…
Where we – among the many travel hither and
yon…and
Who work and live…and play…
And now…where better to be –
Than here at Banff…a respite from –
The hectic-hustle-bustle of everyday-life…and
To be surrounded by family and friend –
And the joy of their presence on…
On this – this June day -
The most significant day in our life –
As We make Our Vows…One to The Other…
And it all –
To be Captured…Encapsulated in
Blessed Ceremony…and Lasting Memory…
In Our Journey Together…and
Into the Future!!

# IN BLOOM

'Does anyone know?'
'Does it show?'
You ask, and with whimsical smile –
Search my face for the answer;
But with chiding and careful banter,
I refuse to satisfy the question.

Just then, and there –
Your friends declare –
It is no secret – it's in the air,
The glint in your face –
Betrays 'the lie';
A flower in bloom –
Always catches the eye.

# SPRING

And the rivulets stream down –
The tear stained mountain-side,
That not too long ago, stood silent,
In its clothing white and cold;
Once more to reveal –
A craggy countenance that –
Tells of times gone by...
Of seasons turbulent and calm,
Their full imprint –
A living testament of aeons gone.

The porous soil gulps of air,
Awaits impeding life to bear,
Of foliage green and flowers fair;
The valley, once more –
To come alive with –
The chitter, chatter, sing-song and twitter,
Of every feathered friend, familiar and strange;
This rejoicing, after the slumber,
To be called, no other name...than, Spring!

# A PEOPLE

The Summer is here – I can feel it
The Summer is here – there's no denying it!
After...the long winter chill – of sucking in,
Every cherished breath – just to be warm...
And not to be frozen still...

I can now hear the rumble and feel...
The rhythm – and to witness the abandon –
The shedding of winter wear of –
Wooly scarves that cluttered throats –
That muffled our sound...
Now give full voice to the being within.

Once cold feet – now thumping the asphalt –
Once gloved hands – now raised heavenward,
With multicoloured palms – fingers spread –
To filter the Summer air – the multitude –
Stomping to the beat!

No snow!  No sleet!
To impede these happy feet –
Infectious laughter – greetings –
And the gyrating 'hereafters' –
The reverberating ping-steel and –
The constant thump of the drum,
All hearken us – to shed our inhibitions –
If only...for a day!

It is an annual yearning – a ritual!
As natural...and as necessary...
As the air we breathe...
A welcome relief from hibernation –

That will now allow the butterflies to soar
Splashing us with glorious colourful splendour!

Needing that space to surface…
Our survival solace…and
To worship at the shrine of Bacchus,
As biblical as our walk to Damascus…
All we need to get through another day.

Hear the drum-beat – the peeling whistles,
Let the bands play on…
Let the many colours of our artistic creations
Drench us – cleanse us of –
The splatter-grimy grey residuals
Of winter's aftermath;
Bring on the smiles and laughter –
That mock the straight-laced,
Who stare in mixed bewilderment – unwilling
To entertain nature's rhythmic inclinations.

Let us be tasteful –
Let us be outrageous –
Let us be tastefully outrageous!
Let us be careful –
Let us be reckless –
Let us be carefully reckless!

Let the people dance…
Let us sing…
These items are not for sale…
Let us all dance…
Let us all sing…
Let us fulfill – what is…
A natural thing…

# AUTUMN

And to watch the falling of the first leaf
Falling...falling...floating...descending...
Drifting reluctantly
Courting every breath of wind
In hopes of staying aloft
Just one moment longer...
To wish a fond farewell to
Some forsaken branch that held it
From the time an infant bud;
Now time to depart...a suckling no longer;
To rest softly in the shade of remaining companions
Soon to be joined in clustered heaps
At the cool base of parental feet.

# FIRST HINT

First hint of winter's snow – when
Tiny flakes – not unlike Spring –
Summer's mischievous mosquitoes –
Flit…and skitter…along the window-pane…
A sign of things to come…
A change that will –
Envelop us…yes!
You…and me!
This pitter-patter against the window.

A teasing…testing our resolve –
Whether to go south – or stay…and
Lean into oncoming winter winds –
That whip the air…
Snowflakes in our hair…
Muffled cloaks and scarves covering us –
Up to here – and above our ear;
Even though a bitter chill…
There's a blessedness…a silence…
That sigh of resignation…
Be still…listen…and hear…
As if there's a tinkling in the air…
A semblance of peace…
That pervades…the atmosphere…
And this…this…
Tranquility…
And so it is…and will be…
For you see…
'Tis the Season!!

# SNOWFLAKE

Each snow-flake seeking its destiny…
Falls unhurriedly from above…
The heavens know alone –
Which square centimeter will be its own –
Falls to the common ground…
Or perched on no particular tree –
More than just a congregation…
Come together in an immaculate body –
Shimmer in the glint –
Reflecting every bit of light –
The once familiar – now in disguise –
On the ground –
Now complete transformation!!
The unimaginable patterns…
The lowly to be crushed underfoot-
Disturbed…removed…
Fresh orientation by you – by me –
It's for our convenience you see!
Listen…and hear…this atmosphere…
Perhaps a message there…
Its position in the scheme of things
Not dependent on punctuality –
But arrives stealthily…
Now will reside at the base of the hill –
And taking its place on the summits…the
Mountain – tops!!
Its particular abode…no matter –
It is here to stay awhile…
The guessing game is done -
It is well within reason…
Some pause in admiration…

For you see... this –
The completion of the year...and –
The Seasons!!

## "DECEMBER 31ST"

It's now closer to six PM…
It's the thirty-first of December –
Almost bitter cold – minus twenty –
And there's magic in the air;
Not many can be seen - on the
Now almost deserted streets –
Sainte Catherine…now –
A respite from the hectic –
Hustle-bustle of holiday crowds;
Now…preparation time!
As we look over our shoulder,
Glancing furtively at yesteryear, and…
As it slowly slips away –
Remembering to recall those who –
Did not 'stay the year' …and
Are not here to share –
The uncertainty – anxiety that –
Titillate our expectancy.

Tonight!  We shall –
Kiss the year goodbye…
And nary a dry eye –
Will be seen, as we
In concert, or alone – unseen,
Shall welcome in…
Hopes of dreams to fulfill –
Menu unseen;
Of demons to conquer –
Of promises to keep -
A slate to 'rub clean' –
A 'fresh start' - a dream,
To come true –

Of faith in me –
Of faith in you;
A challenge to meet -
The dawning of –
Another day...that will –
Take us way into the night...
With secret thoughts...and
Clear eyed ambition;
It is all to our –
Delightful – frightful...
Anticipation...

# ON BE(COM)ING CANADIAN

It is not complete by –
The stroke of the pen…
The signature – the oath…
The anthem;
It is now, only the –
Beginning of a process –
Of time…and circumstance…
Of winters…and seasons ahead,
To shape the mind…
The conscience.
To be conscious of the –
Time and places – the
Vast expansive spaces…
The magnificence and the grandeur…
Of the undulation graces…
It is a process my friend
It is a process…
Of pain and pleasure –
And to each…
Its own measure…

## ODE TO QUÉBEC

October thirty of ninety five
Some Monday...
It's now midnight –
And...
We all...are...still alive...
Very much...alive...
Indistinguishable – and
Together –
Despite our efforts to –
Redefine ourselves,
As tempers flare,
Our teeth to bare, the
Fangs of our –
Pre-historic origins.

And then, as now –
We stake our territory,
To claim our own;
We are distinctly different,
We are indeed...
We are...we are...
Distinctly the same –
Inextinguishable...
Within the castles –
Of our skins.

# ENCORE! MONT-RÉAL...ENCORE!

Now, somewhat dishevelled – and
Countenance stained – the run
Of tearfilled mascara...
That lost, wistful...longing beseeching look...
In eyes that call out –
In syncopated panhandle vernacular,
Unsure...and introspective.

In times gone by...
Inviting all to come in,
From across your bridges, and
From off watery sailing vessels,
Nestling snuggly against,
And hugging your shores...
Swaying rhythmically, slow...
Undulating, the rise-and-fall dance,
And that slap-sound of –
Bottom waters...
That sail ships make.

Your winking city lights,
Silhouetting your magnificent,
Voluptuous contours of night-glow;
Beckoning with that...mystical –
Come hither look of glitter –
That captivates the imagination with,
Promises to offer – as we
In somnambulistic gait – follow...
Misty eyed to the core of -
This fair city...

The hustle-bustle sidewalks,
With reflections in your

Artful décor of window shows
Café sounds of chitter-chatter
Cosmopolitan – an intimacy...
Characteristic of cities –
Multicultural – metropolitan.

Once sophisticated lady,
You embraced the envy –
Of every fair city, when
In fulsome sway, you enticed
Every passing fancy;
Your lively streets,
Infectious laughter...
Your savoir-faire...your,
Oft heard 'bonjour! au revoir'!
'Salut! Merci! à demain!
à la prochaine!'
You...Mont-réal, shall be –
The sophisticated lady of the North again,
Welcoming exotic diversity,
Mont-réal encore!
Encore Mont-réal!
Your intoxicating symphony!
Bonjour! Bonjournée!
Bonsoir! Bonsoirée!
Mont-réal! Mont-réal...
...à votre santé!

# WHEN THEY TAKE YOUR PHOTOGRAPH!

Eyes downcast –
I did suspect, and then made sure,
As the first tear crashed against,
The breast of your freshly pressed jacket,
Of navy blue, and buttons gold.

You sat and leaned against the rack of coats
and almost disappeared, momentarily –
Among the hanging apparel,
Of little persons, such as you -
A sort of withdrawal, I suspect...

And little could I do,
But try to understand your plight,
At the particular moment of quiet despair, as
I knelt before you –
Softly asking your permission,
Whether or not to fasten the button,
Of your coat –
As you softly sobbed –
'Don't worry Daddy' – and I too,
Felt a sudden tug, and unable –
To contain the moisture gathering,
Under the lids.

Just then, your friends came rushing in,
To greet you, for after all...
Your daddy was here!
Unaware that this quiet drama of parting –
Was underway.

Their immediate concern, as they –
On either, and all sides, tried as they might

To see the look in your downcast eyes;
Realizing your slight embarrassment, I said,
'He'll be in, in a minute'
Immediately the dispersal, to me,
Was such a beautiful surprise!

The understanding of young minds,
No insistence on my part, did I make –
And as we emerged from behind –
The cloak-room, coats, hats, scarves et cetera...
You walked briskly to your desk – and,
With accustomed precision –
Removing the chair from atop your desk,
You sat placing your forehead,
Gently upon folded forearms –
Head down, to stem the flow...

You did not see me leave –
So engulfed by teacher, and friends –
Stroking your arms, back and hair –
Saying – 'Don't cry Kyle...'
And as I softly closed the door,
And slowly walked away,
I thought of the way...
You will smile...
When they take your photograph!

# A MOTHER

A time to consider the –
Blessings of a mother...
Who knows of sacrifice...
Who knows of patience...
Who knows of understanding...
Who knows how to be silent...
Who knows when to speak...
Who knows how to heal...
Who knows how not to smother...
Who knows how and when –
And whom, and what –
And when and, where -
And why...
And...why not!
These are the blessings...
Showered on us – by...
A mother!

## SEAN

I never fail to be –
Amazed…
At your diligence,
Tenacity, perspicacity,
Certainly, a gem!
Your vision,
That defies mediocrity.

## MATTHEW

Your choice of career,
Your duty to serve,
Deserves your full attention.
To enforce…is –
To incur resistance,
To uphold…is –
To elicit assistance.

Wherever, and however
You pursue it,
We shall always be there
With you in spirit.

## KYLE

Your steadfastness,
Your thoroughness
Your quiet dignity,
The hallmark –
Dismissive of the
Contrite remark of no import;
As you strive –
Thrive…for family.

# TEARS...JE M'EN SOUVIENS...

The tears we shed – the tears we shared,
Tears – not of deep sorrow, nor grief,
Some relief...and of our parting;
Tears of happiness – sadness, are
Tears of cleansing – from
The source of wells,
Touched at our –
Deepest emotions;
Have no fear...no shame...
A testament to the soul, and
Awakenings of the spirit!

## ON GUARD!

…and with distant gaze,
A landscape to survey…
Framed in the 'V' –
Of a sturdy tree –
On guard – for you! For me!
This Country!

Of the Magnificent #7,
All troops before – those now, and
Then, thereafter –
Duty!  Integrity!
Signature of our security,
All Canadian –
The RCMP!

## "THE THIN LINE"

On hearing 'The thin red line' (Kenneth Alfred)
Its stirring rendition, by the RCMP –
I think of you,
In that smart and,
Significant attire –
Head erect, and
Shoulders square,
To meet the tasks of the day;
To follow tradition of –
A 'Country', true and fair –
CANADA

## 'THE TASK'

Keep the chin up – and
All else falls in line;
A fallen chin, may
Give way to a sagging spirit, for
Then –
Nothing stays in line, but
May give credit
To a fallen spirit;
So…keep the chin up –
My Son (dear one)
And you will be…the better, for it.

## THE POEM

This great experiment in words,
That swims in every head;
These invisible gems that light the souls –
Of the keenest minds and the dullest spirits;
That kindles the faint at heart –
Giving hope to the sinking spirit, or,
With a twist,
Can change a situation –
Resolve an otherwise seemingly hopeless condition.

This experiment in words –
Like a written photograph,
A throbbing symphony,
Could just be the making, or undoing,
Could just be the beginning…the ending –
Could just be the solution –
Could just be the redemption;
Could just be…
This experiment in words…
This litany…this litany,
This great experience in words,
This…the revelation of –
The poem…

# THE LAST POST

A husband – a father,
A grand…and great-grandfather,
And with shoulders square,
He faced the enemy –
Our own mortality…
The battles major and sundry –
Once endured – and
Battles won;

This was the final stage…of –
A soldier in the sun;
Always erect and head –
Held high;
No one could deny…
This was the mark of –
The soldier in him.

And now the shades of night,
Descends on a now peaceful…
Landscape…where –
Many a battle was fought;

We doff our hats…and bow our heads…
In salute!
The day that's done…
And now to rest…
The travails of the world – now
Are none!

## NOTES

A Soldier – forever young! – composed in memory of Private Mascoll MacDonald Best (June 17, 1917 – August 3, 1944) D-135936. Father of Richard M. Best, joined the Canadian Armed Forces and died in Caen, France during World War II.

The Maple Leaf – composed July 1st, 1995 at 8:20pm.

As a Mother would – composed June 17th, 1997

The Outsider – composed a few days after August 7th, 1973

Dream Pillows – composed October 13th, 1996 at 8:20pm.

North Point – composed February 13th, 1973

When? – composed May 8th, 1973

Quintessential Quebecois – composed at Palais de Justice on January 4th, 1995 at 2:10pm.

A Life – composed December 15th, 1994

A Plea – composed July 24th, 1995 at 1:53pm and inspired by "those who serve in the troubled spots of this world".

Once Upon a Time – composed April 12th, 1973

'Bimshire' Beams – composed August 5th, 1975

Y/our Time – composed May 6th, 1995 at 3:08pm.

Truth or Illusion – composed September 24th, 1995 at 8:35pm and inspired listening to Bob Marley and Steel Pulse / True Democracy.

The Party – composed on July 10th, 1973

"I-den-ditty" – composed September 19th, 1997 at 12:05pm.

Caring Hands – composed November 22nd, 2000

Slumber On...– composed in 1975

"The Deep" – composed on August 26th, 1996 at 10:05pm.

'Smokey' – a gentle giant – composed on March 22nd, 2002 at 3:15pm.

NOW – composed August 23rd, 1995 at 10:25am.

An Evening Stroll – composed February 23rd, 1973

Tropic Dusk – composed in 1972

"The High Seas" – composed June 1997 remembering Gerry Roufs who disappeared at sea during the Vendee Globe race around the world.

"Di – almost a Queen and much more" – composed September 3rd, 1997 at 11:25pm inspired by the grace and authenticity of the late Diana Princess of Wales.

In Bloom – composed January 11th, 1973

Spring – composed May 3rd, 1974

A People – composed June 29th, 1996 inspired by "Carifiesta" a colorful parade celebrating the many cultures and traditions from the Caribbean.

Snowflake – composed November 20th, 1972

"December 31st" – composed December 31st, 1996 at 5:40pm.

On Be(Com)ing Canadian – composed January 6th, 1995

Ode to Quebec – composed November 4th, 1995 at 6:45pm downtown Montreal – Peel and Ste. Catherine

Encore! Mont-real…Encore! – composed November 25th, 1995 at 2:21pm.

When They Take Your Photograph! – composed November 3rd, 1978

A Mother – composed May 6th, 2007

Sean Matthew Kyle – composed December 22nd, 1994 at 2:20pm in Toronto, Ontario.

TEARS…Je m'en souviens…– composed August 10th, 1995 at 10:45am while reflecting on the graduating exercises and ceremony of "The Magnificent #7 Troop" of the RCMP in Regina, Saskatchewan.

On Guard! – composed January 4th, 1996

"The Thin Line" – composed January 8th, 1995 for his son, Matthew Best

"The Task" – composed January 8th, 1995

The Poem – composed in 1974

The Last Post – composed July 1st, 2000 in remembering the passing of his Uncle, Major Carlton A. Gardier who served in the Canadian Armed Forces during World War II.

Lightning Source UK Ltd.
Milton Keynes UK
UKHW03f1140260418
321691UK00001B/57/P